Francis Frith's BOGNOR REGIS

PHOTOGRAPHIC MEMORIES

Francis Frith's
BOGNOR REGIS

Martin Andrew

First published in the United Kingdom in 1999 by
Frith Book Company Ltd

Hardback Edition 1999
ISBN 1-85937-055-1

Paperback Edition 2001
ISBN 1-85937-431-x

British Library Cataloguing in Publication Data

Francis Frith's Bognor Regis
Martin Andrew

Frith Book Company Ltd
Frith's Barn, Teffont,
Salisbury, Wiltshire SP3 5QP
Tel: +44 (0) 1722 716 376
Email: info@frithbook.co.uk
www.frithbook.co.uk

Printed and bound in Great Britain

As with any historical database the Frith archive is constantly being corrected and improved and the publishers would welcome information on omissions or inaccuracies

Contents

FRANCIS FRITH: *Victorian Pioneer*

FRANCIS FRITH, Victorian founder of the world-famous photographic archive, was a complex and multitudinous man. A devout Quaker and a highly successful Victorian businessman, he was both philosophic by nature and pioneering in outlook.

By 1855 Francis Frith had already established a wholesale grocery business in Liverpool, and sold it for the astonishing sum of £200,000, which is the equivalent today of over £15,000,000. Now a multi-millionaire, he was able to indulge his passion for travel. As a child he had pored over travel books written by early explorers, and his fancy and imagination had been stirred by family holidays to the sublime mountain regions of Wales and Scotland. 'What a land of spirit-stirring and enriching scenes and places!' he had written. He was to return to these scenes of grandeur in later years to 'recapture the thousands of vivid and tender memories', but with a different purpose. Now in his thirties, and captivated by the new science of photography, Frith set out on a series of pioneering journeys to the Nile regions that occupied him from 1856 until 1860.

INTRIGUE AND ADVENTURE

He took with him on his travels a specially-designed wicker carriage that acted as both dark-room and sleeping chamber. These far-flung journeys were packed with intrigue and adventure. In his life story, written when he was sixty-three, Frith tells of being held captive by bandits, and of fighting 'an awful midnight battle to the very point of surrender with a deadly pack of hungry, wild dogs'. Sporting flowing Arab costume, Frith arrived at Akaba by camel seventy years before Lawrence, where he encountered 'desert princes and rival sheikhs, blazing with jewel-hilted swords'.

During these extraordinary adventures he was assiduously exploring the desert regions bordering the Nile and patiently recording the antiquities and peoples with his camera. He was the first photographer to venture beyond the sixth cataract. Africa was still the mysterious 'Dark Continent', and Stanley and Livingstone's historic meeting was a decade into the future. The conditions for picture taking confound belief. He laboured for hours in his wicker dark-room in the sweltering heat of the desert, while the volatile chemicals fizzed dangerously in their trays. Often he was forced to work in remote tombs and caves where conditions were cooler. Back in London he exhibited his photographs and was 'rapturously cheered' by members of the Royal Society. His reputation as a photographer was made overnight. An eminent modern historian has likened their impact on the population of the time to that on our own generation of the first photographs taken on the surface of the moon.

Venture of a Life-Time

Characteristically, Frith quickly spotted the opportunity to create a new business as a specialist publisher of photographs. He lived in an era of immense and sometimes violent change. For the poor in the early part of Victoria's reign work was a drudge and the hours long, and people had precious little free time to enjoy themselves.

Most had no transport other than a cart or gig at their disposal, and had not travelled far beyond the boundaries of their own town or village. However, by the 1870s, the railways had threaded their way across the country, and Bank Holidays and half-day Saturdays had been made obligatory by Act of Parliament. All of a sudden the ordinary working man and his family were able to enjoy days out and see a little more of the world.

With characteristic business acumen, Francis Frith foresaw that these new tourists would enjoy having souvenirs to commemorate their days out. In 1860 he married Mary Ann Rosling and set out with the intention of photographing every city, town and village in Britain. For the next thirty years he travelled the country by train and by pony and trap, producing fine photographs of seaside resorts and beauty spots that were keenly bought by millions of Victorians. These prints were painstakingly pasted into family albums and pored over during the dark nights of winter, rekindling precious memories of summer excursions.

The Rise of Frith & Co

Frith's studio was soon supplying retail shops all over the country. To meet the demand he gathered about him a small team of photographers, and published the work of independent artist-photographers of the calibre of Roger Fenton and Francis Bedford. In order to gain some understanding of the scale of Frith's business one only has to look at the catalogue issued by Frith & Co in 1886: it runs to some 670

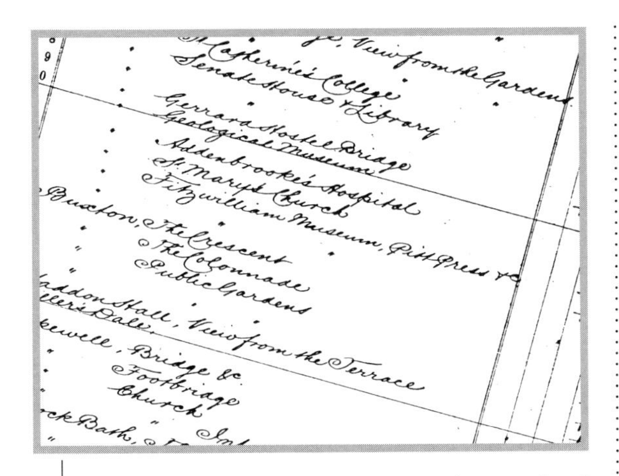
View from the Gardens
Catherine's College
Senate House & Library
Gerrard Hostel Bridge
Geological Museum
Addenbrooke's Hospital
St Mary's Church
Fitzwilliam Museum, Pitt Press &c
Buxton, The Crescent
The Colonnade
Public Gardens
Haddon Hall, View from the Terrace
Millers Dale
Bakewell, Bridge &c
Footbridge
Church

pages, listing not only many thousands of views of the British Isles but also many photographs of most European countries, and China, Japan, the USA and Canada – note the sample page shown above from the hand-written *Frith & Co* ledgers detailing pictures taken. By 1890 Frith had created the greatest specialist photographic publishing company in the world, with over 2,000 outlets – more than the combined number that Boots and WH Smith have today! The picture on the right shows the *Frith & Co* display board at Ingleton in the Yorkshire Dales. Beautifully constructed with mahogany frame and gilt inserts, it could display up to a dozen local scenes.

Postcard Bonanza

The ever-popular holiday postcard we know today took many years to develop. In 1870 the Post Office issued the first plain cards, with a pre-printed stamp on one face. In 1894 they allowed other publishers' cards to be sent through the mail with an attached adhesive halfpenny stamp. Demand grew rapidly, and in 1895 a new size of postcard was permitted called the court card, but there was little room for illustration. In 1899, a year after Frith's death, a new card measuring 5.5 x 3.5 inches became the standard format, but it was not until 1902 that the divided back came into being, with address and message on one face and a full-size illustration on the other. *Frith & Co* were in the vanguard of postcard development, and Frith's sons Eustace and Cyril continued their father's monumental task, expanding the number of views offered to the public and recording more and more places in Britain, as the coasts and countryside were opened up to mass travel.

Francis Frith died in 1898 at his villa in Cannes, his great project still growing. The archive he created continued in business for another seventy years. By 1970 it contained over a third of a million pictures of 7,000 cities, towns and villages. The massive photographic record Frith has left to us stands as a living monument to a special and very remarkable man.

Frith's Archive: *A Unique Legacy*

Francis Frith's legacy to us today is of immense significance and value, for the magnificent archive of evocative photographs he created provides a unique record of change in 7,000 cities, towns and villages throughout Britain over a century and more. Frith and his fellow studio photographers revisited locations many times down the years to update their views, compiling for us an enthralling and colourful pageant of British life and character.

We tend to think of Frith's sepia views of Britain as nostalgic, for most of us use them to conjure up memories of places in our own lives with which we have family associations. It often makes us forget that to Francis Frith they were records of daily life as it was actually being lived in the cities, towns and villages of his day. The Victorian age was one of great and often bewildering change for ordinary people, and though the pictures evoke an impression of slower times, life was as busy and hectic as it is today.

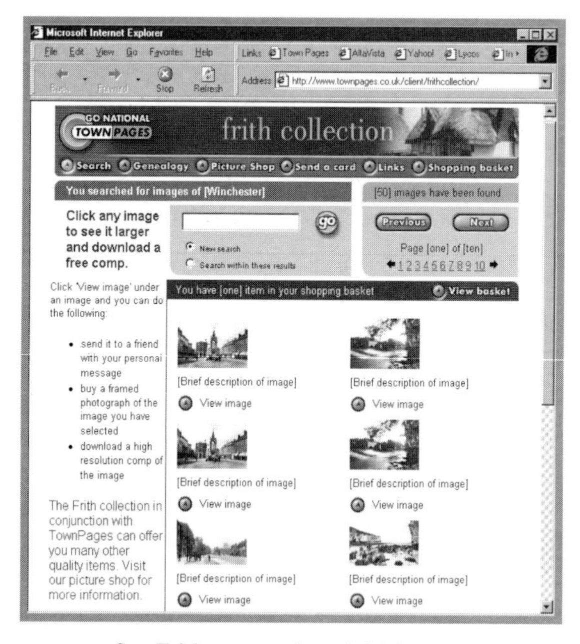

See Frith at www. francisfrith.co.uk

We are fortunate that Frith was a photographer of the people, dedicated to recording the minutiae of everyday life. For it is this sheer wealth of visual data, the painstaking chronicle of changes in dress, transport, street layouts, buildings, housing, engineering and landscape that captivates us so much today. His remarkable images offer us a powerful link with the past and with the lives of our ancestors.

Today's Technology

Computers have now made it possible for Frith's many thousands of images to be accessed almost instantly. In the Frith archive today, each photograph is carefully 'digitised' then stored on a CD Rom. Frith archivists can locate a single photograph amongst thousands within seconds. Views can be catalogued and sorted under a variety of categories of place and content to the immediate benefit of researchers. Inexpensive reference prints can be created for them at the touch of a mouse button, and a wide range of books and other printed materials assembled and published for a wider, more general readership - in the next twelve months over a hundred Frith local history titles will be published! The day-to-day workings of the archive are very different from how they were in Francis Frith's time: imagine the herculean task of sorting through eleven tons of glass negatives as Frith had to do to locate a particular sequence of pictures! Yet the archive still prides itself on maintaining the same high standards of excellence laid down by Francis Frith, including the painstaking cataloguing and indexing of every view.

It is curious to reflect on how the internet now allows researchers in America and elsewhere greater instant access to the archive than Frith himself ever enjoyed. Many thousands of individual views can be called up on screen within seconds on one of the Frith internet sites, enabling people living continents away to revisit the streets of their ancestral home town, or view places in Britain where they have enjoyed holidays. Many overseas researchers welcome the chance to view special theme selections, such as transport, sports, costume and ancient monuments.

We are certain that Francis Frith would have heartily approved of these modern developments, for he himself was always working at the very limits of Victorian photographic technology.

The Value of the Archive Today

Because of the benefits brought by the computer, Frith's images are increasingly studied by social historians, by researchers into genealogy and ancestry, by architects, town planners, and by teachers and schoolchildren involved in local history projects. In addition, the archive offers every one of us a unique opportunity to examine the places where we and our families have lived and worked down the years. Immensely successful in Frith's own era, the archive is now, a century and more on, entering a new phase of popularity.

The Past in Tune with the Future

Historians consider the Francis Frith Collection to be of prime national importance. It is the only archive of its kind remaining in private ownership and has been valued at a million pounds. However, this figure is now rapidly increasing as digital technology enables more and more people around the world to enjoy its benefits.

Francis Frith's archive is now housed in an historic timber barn in the beautiful village of Teffont in Wiltshire. Its founder would not recognize the archive office as it is today. In place of the many thousands of dusty boxes containing glass plate negatives and an all-pervading odour of photographic chemicals, there are now ranks of computer screens. He would be amazed to watch his images travelling round the world at unimaginable speeds through network and internet lines.

The archive's future is both bright and exciting. Francis Frith, with his unshakeable belief in making photographs available to the greatest number of people, would undoubtedly approve of what is being done today with his lifetime's work. His photographs, depicting our shared past, are now bringing pleasure and enlightenment to millions around the world a century and more after his death.

BOGNOR REGIS – *An Introduction*

FROM HOTHAMPTON TO BOGNOR REGIS: A SEASIDE STORY.

AN ENTRY in the parish register of St Mary Magdalene Parish Church at South Bersted records the laying of the first stone of a public bathing place by Sir Richard Hotham at The Lodge, Bognor, on 18 January 1787. This was effectively the beginning of the seaside resort of Bognor. It then lay within the boundaries of Bersted parish, the shingled spire of whose parish church can be glimpsed beyond the Bognor Regis War Memorial Hospital, just north of the Chichester Road.

From the ambitions of this wealthy London hatter, Bognor (then a few fishermen's cottages with a small chapel of ease and notorious for smuggling) grew into one of the south coast of England's major seaside resorts. Architecturally it remains a less coherent resort than many, for Hotham's scheme never quite came to full fruition, and nor did many other further entrepreneurial initiatives. Thus, despite Hotham's aim of 'making Bognor the resort of more select company than is to be found at other bathing places', it never quite made the grade. Most of Bognor as a resort was cheerful and friendly, rather than stuffy and stand-offish like, say, Eastbourne or Hove. Despite this, it also had select areas, and after King George V had recuperated here at Craigwell House from a very serious lung infection in 1929 it was granted the right to add 'Regis', meaning 'of the king' or 'royal', to its name. This goes slightly counter to the no doubt apocryphal tale that King George V's last words in 1936 were 'Bugger Bognor'.

It was always popular with day trippers who flooded in by railway, and in 1960 Butlins opened its holiday camp to the east of the town. By this time Bognor and its council were desperate to modernise: much of the best of the old town disappeared under the bulldozer. Thus these 'Photographic Memories' tend depressingly to be just that in terms of historic Bognor.

In 1784, however, all this was in the future. Sir Richard Hotham's ambitious plan for his 1600 acre estate did not intend to cater for the common herd. He poured his £100,000 fortune into the project, perhaps £7,000,000 in today's money. For himself he built Chapel House (or The Lodge or Chapel Lodge), set in generous parkland. It is now called Hotham House and sits amid Hotham Park which, probably to the posthumous horror of Sir Richard, is a public park with mini-golf, a mini-railway line threading through his parkland trees, refreshment kiosks and formerly a full-blown zoo with an elephant. His chapel was demolished as long ago as 1859, but the tower with its clock survives, attached to the rear of Hotham House, which has finally emerged safely converted to flats after years of underuse and minimal repair.

North of the park Hotham built terraces and houses along the Upper Bognor Road. Quite some distance from the sea, these were included dukes and other aristocrats as well as the prosperous middle class. For example, in 1796 the Countess of Jersey rented Dome House, and was visited by the Prince of Wales, later the Prince Regent, during her stay. After Hotham's death Princess Charlotte, the Prince Regent's daughter, spent her summers in Dome House from 1808 to 1811, and the future Queen Victoria stayed as a child at what is now Hotham House for several summers between 1821 and 1830.

Further south, Hotham laid out Waterloo Square (as it is called now - Hotham immodestly named it Hotham Fields) and built at its north end two fine terraces of houses,

intended to be highly select. By becoming a college of education, they survived the town's demolition frenzy. The finest was Dome House in The Crescent, a brick house of about 1790, flanked by stucco terraces. Further west, beyond Mead Lane, were more large terrace houses in brick or stucco, known originally as Spencer Terrace. By Sir Richard's death in 1799 he had succeeded so far as to have the houses rented in the summer for up to eleven guineas a week, and the tenants Hothampton Place and East Row. Unfortunately, these have been demolished, but at least the bulk of Hotham's planning for 'Hothampton' survived as the skeleton for later schemes and expansions. By the time he died in 1799, his successes were matched by his failures, but many hoped to build on his achievement of noble patronage combined with high quality housing.

For example, Daniel Wonham built Rock Buildings, a crescent of eleven three storey stucco houses, west of the old library: others built villas along the north side of what is now the High Street, but was then called Bedford Row. But there was no effective master planning for Bognor's growth in the nineteenth century: the Royal Norfolk Hotel was built in its present location after the earlier one, east of Rock Buildings, burnt down in 1826, while Mr Binstead's first library nearer the sea gave up and moved inland in 1823 - the sea-battered house was demolished.

The Steyne developed in the 1820s, its name copied from Brighton, and buildings started to line the east and west sides of Waterloo Square. Mostly these were of a smaller and more cottagey Regency style, with Waterloo balconies on most of them. They were very much of a lesser grandeur than Hotham's building work, and contributed to the curious and wide variations in building styles in the town as it evolved. This informality and intimacy became one of its greatest assets and a source of its very widespread appeal, but it did produce some curious architectural anomalies. Perhaps this very odd cheek-by-jowl mixture of grand housing with cottages assisted the modern demolition fever, for Bognor never had the homogeneous uniformity of an Eastbourne or a St Leonards.

In 1826, further east along the shore, the noted architect Samuel Beazley built another shallow crescent of four pairs of semi-detached stuccoed houses of a quality worthy of Cheltenham. They and Rock Buildings were demolished this century. By 1870, Bognor, to judge from old prints and engravings, had achieved a good seaside development based on Waterloo Square and the Steyne, spreading west and east along the shore as well as inland.

Two other factors led to further growth: one was inevitably the railway, the other the pier. The first almost did not arrive, as the Worthing to Chichester line passed over three miles to the north in 1845. Nothing daunted, a station was built at Woodgate where the line crossed the London to Bognor road, and there the sign 'Bognor Station' duly appeared. Until 1862, when a branch was opened from Barnham Junction to Bognor, visitors had a coach ride from the little country station at Woodgate. The arrival of the railway led to a further acceleration of Bognor's growth, and in May 1865 Queen Victoria's 'dear little Bognor' acquired a 1000-foot long pier, extending into the sea from the axis of the mid point of Waterloo Square.

To exploit the easier access new development arrived, including the grand Park Terrace to the west and large numbers of villas elsewhere. But yet again grand schemes stumbled. From the pier you can see The Carlton Hotel to the north-east. This started with great expectations, the foundation stone being laid in 1880 by Lord William Pitt Lennox. This four storey cement-rendered building has six bays to its front and then four curved bays to the right. It looks odd now, but was intended as the start of a vast crescent over 600 feet long which would have given Bognor something very special for its seafront. However, the company collapsed, and only this incongruously high and stolid Italianate fragment of great ambitions remains.

In many of the views in this book, bathing machines can be seen, a common sight in all seaside resorts until after the First World War. They were in effect mobile changing rooms hauled into the sea to a suitable depth by a horse. The occupant could then emerge modestly down the steps to bathe. Bognor had initially about a dozen, but the numbers waxed and waned. The most famous bathing machine attendant was Mary Wheatland, who had her pitch with over a dozen machines occupying a prime site on the east side of the pier. She was a well-known character from the late Victorian years until the 1920s.

Bognor remained very popular throughout most of the 20th century for family holidays, only really finding the going tough when the cheap overseas package holiday arrived. Butlins, opened in 1960, remains a key element in the town's success, having undergone a variety of re-vampings over the years. Back in the Edwardian period, the town gained The Arcade, a glass-roofed shopping mall, and, in 1910, the Kursaal. Both were developed by the local entrepreneur William Tate; the Kursaal took its name from the main buildings in German spa towns and watering places, the 'cure hall'. Tate copied the name from Eastbourne's Kursaal which had been built on their pier in 1899, and in it he provided a theatre, a skating rink, a constitutional club, shops and tea rooms. Very much a landmark along the shore with its domed corner towers, it assumed the less distinguished name of the Rex Entertainment Centre in 1947. Its demolition in 1975 coincided with a period when the town was in the doldrums, and it took some time for a replacement entertainment centre to emerge, the depressingly drab yellow brick Regis Centre.

After the Second World War the council set about doing what Hitler had failed to achieve. Demolition mania had started before the War in 1935 when Hothampton Place was demolished: it is hard to believe that the reason was that it was blocking views of the frontage of the Pavilion dance hall. In 1947 the council shamefully demolished Beazley's Colebrook Terrace for reasons unknown: its site is still merely a car park. Hotham House

itself narrowly escaped demolition, East Row went in 1955, and Rock Buildings as recently as 1980. The Kursaal, as we saw, went in 1975. The villas on the north side of the High Street west of London Road went, and the trail of destruction saw the Esplanade Theatre go in 1980, St John's Parish Church and vicarage in London Road in 1975, the Surrey Women's Convalescent Home in 1980 ... the list goes on.

What replaced much of this was mediocrity and nowheres-ville; the Queensway development, which was intended to regenerate the shopping centre, combined lumpy 1960s buildings with a far too high tower block of flats intrusive for miles around. To make matters worse, the tower block usurped the name that East Row had acquired in the nineteenth century: Fitzleet House. Rock Buildings and the Surrey Women's Convalescent Home were replaced by very large and dull blocks of flats, as was the Beaulieu Hotel. I hope the tide has now turned: what remains of Hothampton seems safe, and The Steyne and Waterloo Square, and the intimate streets around that area as far as West Street, have survived well, and with luck will continue to do so.

Bognor Regis must continue to adapt and change, but it is hoped that more sense of the value of the buildings that made the town such an attractive and eclectic mix will prevail. Much of what is shown in this book does remain as a cultural backbone for the town. It still has a unique character, but not one Sir Richard Hotham would recognise: it is friendly, slightly kiss-me-quick-hatted in some ways, but it also has pockets of elegance. Around The Steyne area you can still get much of the original feeling of the town as a Victorian seaside resort: a feeling now lost east of the Carlton Hotel along the foreshore.

I like Bognor, and have known it for over thirty years, but it was only when I came to research this book that I realised how much of its historic fabric had gone, some of it as recently as the 1980s. This book will give you a fascinating picture of how this holiday town evolved and has changed, and I hope you enjoy looking again at Bognor Regis as much as I have.

South Bersted, The Church And Vicarage 1898 42596
Bognor was in Bersted parish until 1873. The medieval church with its broach spire is seen in this view from the field in which the Bognor Regis War Memorial Hospital was built after World War I and recently rebuilt. The vicarage beyond has succumbed to a housing estate.

Felpham, St Mary's Church 1890 25192
A mile east of Bognor the village of Felpham is separated from the town only by Butlins holiday camp. It too has a good medieval church, but this view from the south is now blocked by Gateway Lodge, modern houses and flats, but some of the flint walling survives.

HOTHAM HOUSE c1955 B130094

Several of Sir Richard Hotham's 'Hothampton' houses survive: this is Hotham House, whose grounds, Hotham Park, have been a public park since 1947, complete with a narrow gauge railway. The house was built in 1792, and Hotham lived here until his death in 1799. The tower is all that remains of his chapel.

HOTHAMPTON PLACE 1895 36264
The first terrace built by Hotham in the 1780s: it stood at the north end of his Hothampton (now Waterloo) Square. Sold to The Merchant Taylors as a ladies' home in 1870, it was unfortunately demolished in 1935 to create a forecourt for the Dance Pavilion, itself demolished in 1949.

MERCHANT TAYLORS HOME, HIGH STREET, SOUTH FRONT 1898 42594
Immediately east of Hothampton Place, Hotham built East Row in the 1790s. After 1870, it became a convalescent home for male members of The Merchant Taylors Company. Like many houses in Bognor, it was stuccoed using cement produced at the Black Mill, a now-demolished windmill situated in nearby Nyewood Lane

London Road
by Hotham Park 1903 50206
A much changed view, although the houses on the right survive. On the left in what was part of Hotham's estate is now a primary school and public library, whose grounds retain this openness. The wall in the middle distance hides Hotham's 1792 ice house, now bereft of its earth mound.

MERCHANT TAYLORS HOME, HIGH STREET, NORTH FRONT 1898 42593
The north or rear elevation of Fitzleet House, as East Row was renamed when it became a single house in the early nineteenth century, was plainer, its centre dominated by the tall staircase window. To the right a Gothic-styled flint chapel was built by the Merchant Taylors.

UPPER BOGNOR ROAD, HOTHAM PARK 1895 35133
The trees and flint wall on the right hide The Crescent, Hotham's most ambitious buildings, while the road junction is that with the High Street. Beyond is the old lodge, demolished about 1900, and gates to Hotham Park. Behind the trees on the left, some of which survive, is Butlins holiday camp.

Upper Bognor Road 1903 50208
Looking east to the High Street junction, the wall on the right forms the north boundary to Hotham Park. Although the wall survives, the magnificent trees have long gone, and the road is now a very busy one.

UPPER BOGNOR ROAD 1903 50209

This view shows the front boundary wall to Niagara House, a stucco villa of about 1800. Beyond Mead Lane are the walls fronting the grounds of The Crescent, a development that includes The Dome of about 1790, all now a further education college.

HIGH STREET, LOOKING WEST 1914 66932

HIGH STREET
Looking West 1914

On the right, Staley's department store, now Bobby's, on the corner of London Road, had just been built in 1914. Many of the nineteenth century buildings on the left survive, albeit now dominated by the tall 1930s Reynolds, a local firm that had outgrown its two Regency shops.

HIGH STREET, LOOKING WEST 1914 66932A

POST OFFICE.
LONG & STRICKLAND.

High Street

Looking West 1890 22633

In this view from the corner of York Road, the right hand side of the road is now utterly changed. The Regency villas of Bedford Row survived into the 1930s when the splendid tile-fronted Art Deco 'Southdown' bus station (now itself demolished) swept some of them away: the rest followed.

ALL
KODAK
SUPPLIES
LAWRENCE WOOD
KODAK
SPECIALIST
BP 2357

HIGH STREET

Looking West 1914 66933

In this view, again from the corner of York Road, the 1830s stuccoed terrace was one of the best buildings on the High Street, although its pediment and cornice have now been simplified. Beyond, the scale is somewhat jumbled, and several buildings have been replaced - and not for the better.

HIGH STREET, LOOKING EAST 1914 66934

HIGH STREET, LOOKING EAST 1914 66934A

HIGH STREET
Looking East 1914
The library building, here Webster and Webb's (and now Mann's estate agents), was founded by Robert Knapton in the early 1820s to provide reading material for visitors to Bognor, some of them royal. It is a distinguished Regency building erected opposite the gate piers to Hotham's now demolished East Row, later Fitzleet House.

St John's Parish Church, Interior 1898 42592
Arthur Blomfield's 1882 church on London Road was demolished in 1975 to make way for Mammon in the shape of Boots and W.H.Smith's large red brick building. Its spire, only completed in 1895, dominated views in London Road, now a pedestrianised shopping street.

SUDELEY ROAD 1903 50205

The fine range of Victorian semi-detached villas on the right survive, now mostly offices, and the flint wall on the left is also largely intact, although punctured by vehicle accesses. However, the huge vicarage and St John's Church (out of picture on the left) went in 1975, their plot filled by the new Smiths and Boots building.

The Steyne 1895 36260

The Steyne
1895

Named after The Steyne in fashionable Brighton, this long, narrow square was laid out in the 1820s and is lined by modest seaside houses, many with balconies and verandahs. No.9, on the far left, was built in 1824 as the bath house; here, salt water baths could be taken in the basement.

The Steyne 1895 36260A

Looking North-West from the Pier
c1880 22627
Bognor acquired a sea wall and promenade partly for the benefits of promenaders but mainly to protect the land from the rapidly encroaching sea. In 1865 the 1000-foot pier opened, which became a favourite spot for photographers: here we are looking at the seafront buildings before the ornate Royal Hotel was built.

THE PARADE, LOOKING EAST 1890 22629

THE PARADE, LOOKING EAST 1890 22629A

THE PARADE
Looking East 1890

This view, with the pier in the background, shows the 1840s Marine Parade behind the Esplanade Gardens. Beyond are Rock Buildings, a crescent of eleven houses built in 1804 by Daniel Wonham, inexplicably demolished in 1980 and replaced by Rock Gardens, six storey blocks of flats.

The Parade, Looking East 1892 29973
To the left is The Royal Norfolk Hotel, by now with its cast-iron balconies, and the ornate arch into the Esplanade Park, now gone; the park is now dedicated to skate boarders. Beyond are the buildings along the east side of West Street.

Norfolk Hotel 1890 22630
Now enlarged by five bays to the left and four to the right, with a fine central cast-iron balcony, with architraves and pediments added to the windows, and renamed The Royal Norfolk Hotel, one of Bognor's best buildings was rebuilt here after the original burned down in 1826.

PARK TERRACE
1890 22635
Situated west of Marine Parade, Park Terrace dates from the 1870s, and was popular with the nobility and well-to-do, including the Duke of Portland who owned one of the houses. These houses carry the Regency love of first-floor Waterloo balconies over into the context of the more stolid High Victorian architecture.

THE PARADE, EAST OF THE PIER 1892 29972
To the east of the pier this quiet view along what was then called Gloucester Promenade, now The Esplanade, shows the pier before any buildings were added; to the right stands The Carlton Hotel, the remnant of an ambitious crescent that never got any further.

FROM THE PIER, LOOKING NORTH-EAST 1890 22626
Until the 1920s these bathing machines were ready for business at 6 am with 'the conductor waiting', and were 'drawn (by a horse) to any depth required; at low water the bather may even go as far as the rocks; the ladies will find a female guide'.

The Beach from the Pier 1890 22624
Again taken from the pier, this view shows the east side of Waterloo Square with, behind the flag-flying Beach Hotel, the cupola'd bell tower of the old fire station which moved inland in about 1900.

From the Pier

Rough Seas 1890 25182B

Rough seas were always popular with local photographers; this photograph shows a spectacular sea crashing over the promenade to batter the Carlton Hotel. Such views were Victorian and Edwardian postcard best-sellers, and those by the local photographer, W.P.Marsh, were particularly prized.

THE BEACH HOTEL 1898 42584
In the foreground is one of the horses whose job was to haul the bathing machines in and out of the sea. Beyond The Beach Hotel and The Carlton Hotel, the white building is the end of Colebrooke Buildings, a crescent of four elegant Regency semi-detached villas built in 1826.

ARTHUR'S HOUSE, ALDWICK ROAD 1898 42595
Arthur's Convalescent Home, now Ashley House, a Shaftesbury Home, was built in the 1890s as a convalescent home, one of a number built for those recovering from illness to take benefit from the bracing sea air. Distinguished by its battlemented tower, it is in the then up-to-the-minute Arts and Crafts style.

The Pier 1911 63786

The Pier
1911
By 1911, the pier has acquired an agglomeration of buildings at the landward end to replace the elegant 1865 entrance kiosk with its ogee pyramidal roof. They were built by the Bognor Pier Company who bought the pier from the council in 1909; they contained a cinema, a theatre and arcades of shops.

The Pier 1911 63786A

THE DIAMOND JUBILEE DRINKING FOUNTAIN AND THE PIER 1921 71438
The drinking fountain in fine pink, grey and green granites was erected here on the promenade south of The Steyne in 1898, commemorating Queen Victoria's Diamond Jubilee. It was moved to Waterloo Square before finally ending up in the Steyne in 1969.

FROM THE PIER, LOOKING NORTH-WEST 1903 50182

FROM THE PIER
Looking North-West 1903
In this view the grand Royal Hotel, with its array of verandahs and balconies, built about 1880 by a Mr Arthur Smith, dominates the earlier Regency stucco all around. In the middle distance is the 1830s Steyne Cottage Hotel, and on the far left Rock Buildings.

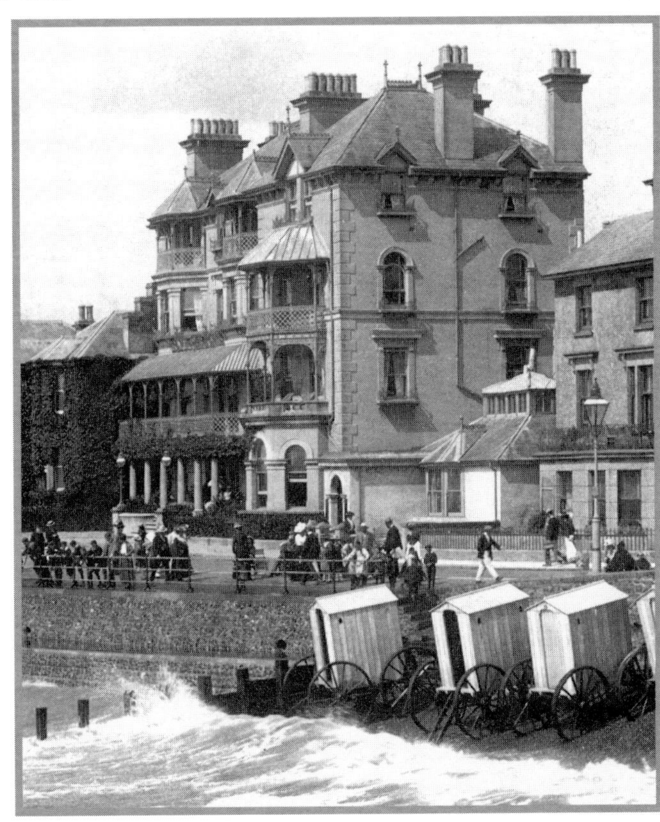

FROM THE PIER, LOOKING NORTH-WEST 1903 50182A

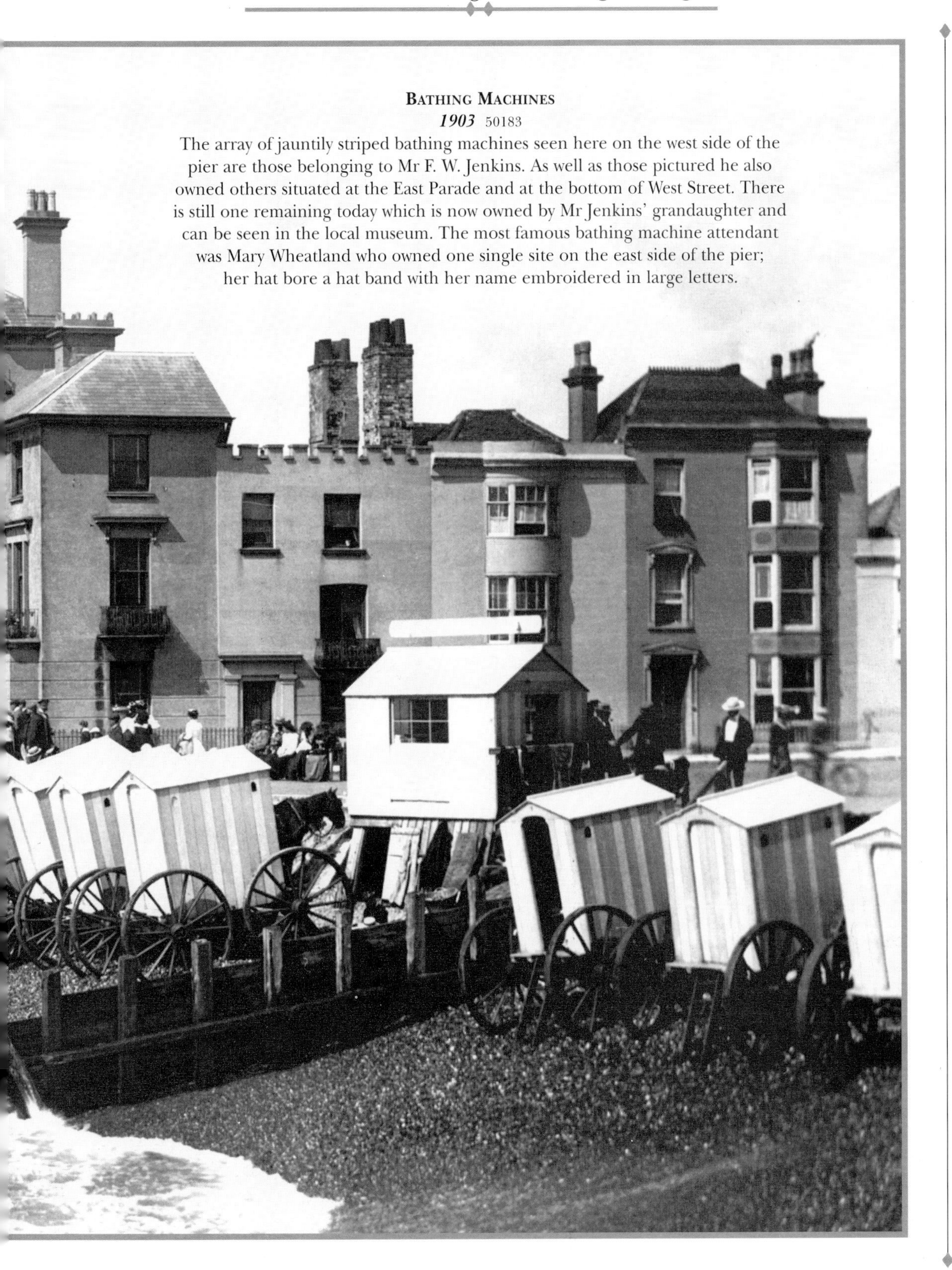

BATHING MACHINES
1903 50183
The array of jauntily striped bathing machines seen here on the west side of the pier are those belonging to Mr F. W. Jenkins. As well as those pictured he also owned others situated at the East Parade and at the bottom of West Street. There is still one remaining today which is now owned by Mr Jenkins' grandaughter and can be seen in the local museum. The most famous bathing machine attendant was Mary Wheatland who owned one single site on the east side of the pier; her hat bore a hat band with her name embroidered in large letters.

THE PARADE AND THE PIER 1911 63790
The Ancient Mariner Hotel on the corner of West Street and Lansdowne House beyond have, sad to say, lost their balconies, but the buildings remain. In the foreground genteel holiday makers make their dignified way along the promenade.

FROM THE PIER, LOOKING WEST 1914 66935

FROM THE PIER
Looking West 1914
Taken from high up on the pier buildings, this view shows the Promenade as far as the West Bandstand, erected in 1901 and enlarged in 1910, in the Esplanade Gardens. Behind are Rock Buildings, which form a foreground to the taller mass of Park Terrace.

FROM THE PIER, LOOKING WEST 1914 66935A

THE CENTRAL RESTAURANT
WATERLOO INN
THE CENTRAL RESTAURANT

Waterloo Square

Sheep Grazing 1921 71443

Waterloo Square, until about 1815 called Hothampton Field, was planned by Sir Richard Hotham in the 1780s and remained a grassy sward, evenly cropped by sheep, into the 1920s. Since then the town has owned it; it is now a welter of municipal gardens, bowling greens and high hedges.

THE PARADE 1906 56733
Further west were the Esplanade Gardens, entered through the cast iron arch supporting the lamp. Within was the bandstand, erected in 1901 at the modest cost of £60. Behind are Rock Buildings, Daniel Wonham's shallow crescent of eleven dignified 1804 villas.

WEST PARADE 1903 50187
Genteel Park Terrace overlooks West Parade; its walls remain, although the sea wall itself has been recently rebuilt. In the distance, beyond the stucco of Marine Parade, the view is now dominated by Rock Gardens: 1980s brick six-storey blocks of flats, inferior but aggressive replacements for the Regency stucco Rock Buildings.

PARK TERRACE 1903 50201
Since the earlier view of about 1890, the terrace has matured and the gardens in front have been set out. The terrace, built as eight houses, is now divided into three blocks of flats: Sussex Court, Lyndhurst Court in the middle and Elizabeth Court on the right.

West Parade
Looking East 1906 56737
This view gives a good impression of a windy seaside holiday: The beach tents billow, and the nannies' aprons billow too as they push their perambulators, one hand clutching their hats. The pier end pavilion seen on the right was added in 1900, and washed into the sea in 1965.

THE
DINING&TEA
RESTAURANT
DINING&TEA ROOMS
WILMOTT
ESTABLISHED 1875

From the Pier
Looking North-East 1903 50184
Behind the Beach Hotel, between it and the old fire station tower, are the premises of the noted local photographer, W.P.Marsh; the fire station itself is now advertising Cycles for Hire. Further left, in recently erected houses, is the curiously-named 'People's Dining and Tea Rooms'.

VIEW FROM THE PIER 1906 56732

VIEW FROM THE PIER 1906 56732A

VIEW FROM THE PIER
1906

The low buildings between The Beach Hotel and The Carlton Hotel, on the right, are now replaced by the Cassino, a four-storey 1990s fake stucco seaside-style building with octagonal corner towers and a central gabled bay with skinny balconies in between.

THE PARADE, FROM THE PIER 1914 66944

THE PARADE
From the Pier 1914

By 1914 The Beach Hotel has been modernised by the addition of a fourth storey, while the front bay windows have also been raised by a storey; the stucco has been painted a darker colour. To the left, the photographer's studio has gone and a smart bay window has been added.

THE PARADE, FROM THE PIER 1914 66944A

EAST PARADE 1921 71433
Everything to the right of the Carlton Hotel has now been demolished, but many of the buildings will be looked at in other views in the book. The bus driver is posing proudly beside his bus.

The Parade, Cotswold Crescent 1903 50193

The Parade
Cotswold Crescent 1903
The foundation stone of the Carlton Hotel on the right was laid by Lord William Pitt Lennox on 8 July 1880. Cotswold Crescent was intended to be the start of a crescent with a frontage of over 600 feet, but only the left end and first four bays of the crescent were ever completed.

The Parade, Cotswold Crescent 1903 50193A

EAST PARADE AND THE PIER
1911 63793

Viewed from further east, the truncated Cotswold Crescent now has a partner, The Beaulieu Hotel, erected in 1908 in a totally different style: a sort of seaside Queen Anne, with two storeys of verandahs, which looks curiously squat and uncomfortable next to the tall Italianate Carlton Hotel.

THE KURSAAL 1914 66946
In 1910 the ambitious local entrepreneur William Tate built the Kursaal. Eastbourne had built a Kursaal on its pier in 1899, and he liked the name's healthy ring: it came from German spa towns, and literally means 'cure hall'. Inside was a theatre, a skating rink, shops and tea rooms.

EAST PARADE 1903 50191

These two pairs of refined stucco Regency semi-detached villas were part of Colebrooke Terrace, a shallow crescent of four pairs. They were built in 1826 to designs by Samuel Beazley, who also built the Theatre Royal in Dublin. These were among the finest sea front houses in Bognor.

EAST PARADE AND THE KURSAAL 1911 63795

In 1910 Beazley's villas acquired a brash new neighbour: the Kursaal, with its octagonal domed towers and second floor balcony. The Kursaal was renamed the Rex Entertainment Centre in 1947: a far less stylish name, but perhaps more appropriate for the modern age.

EAST PARADE 1921 71434
Beazley's Colebrooke Terrace was started on 24th September 1824; three hundred workmen were employed. It was then unoriginally named New Crescent. The pair on the right became Colebrooke House School for Boys, founded by a chairman of Bognor Council, the very council that demolished the terrace in 1947.

COLEBROOKE TERRACE 1908 50190
This view shows the subtle curve of Colebrooke Terrace. The end building was The Royal Clarence Hotel, one of the most expensive in Bognor. The terrace was crassly all demolished in 1947; the site is now merely a car park for the Regis Centre.

East Parade, the Kursaal 1911 63794

This view, in which only the piers and bastion of the promenade on the right now survive, shows the grand Italianate design of the Kursaal well: its loss in 1975 was tragic, and its replacement, the dreary yellow brick Regis Centre, is not a worthy successor to such a striking building.

Colebrooke Terrace 1921 71430

The right pair of the 1820s Colebrooke Terrace was larger than the other pairs, and further differentiated by a two-storey bow window to its centre, as befitted The Royal Clarence Hotel.

THE PARADE, LOOKING WEST 1921 71429

THE PARADE, LOOKING WEST 1921 71429A

THE PARADE
Looking West 1921
This photograph is taken further east beyond Colebrooke Crescent. In the foreground is the Jacobean-style Surrey Convalescent Home for Women, demolished in 1980 and replaced by more flats, Berkeley Court. As in many views in this book, there are cumbersome-looking perambulators on the prom giving babies the benefits of sea air.

Surrey Convalescent Home for Women 1900 46118

Also known as The Princess Mary Memorial Home and Victorian Convalescent Home for Surrey Women, the home was opened by Princess Alexandra of Teck on 4 April 1906. The loss in 1980 of its dignified Jacobean architecture was another Bognor mistake: a surprisingly late one in these more conservationist days.

Aldwick, The Bathing Beach 1903 50199

South of Marine Gardens and further west along the coast, there were many bathing huts of all shapes and sizes on Aldwick's beach. There are still quite a few nowadays. Beyond are the scrub and tree-covered areas of the Pagham Harbour Nature Reserve, a beautiful spot and a noted birdwatching area.

EAST PARADE

1903 50189

In this view there is little development near the sea at this stage in Bognor's growth. The right hand building survives as part of Field House on the corner of Gloucester Road. Beyond the marshy flats where the Aldingbourne Rife reaches the sea, the land remained undeveloped until Butlins arrived in 1960.

WATERLOO SQUARE

From the Pier 1955 B130073

This view captures well the 1950s bustle of the seaside resort with the cafes and amusement arcades along the east side of Waterloo Square. Also it shows how the Square was divided up, with the area beyond the gardens a hedged-off enclosure for two bowling greens.

PIER
GARAGE
WALLS RESTAURANT
WALLS RESTAURANT
SAIT & GALE
ENGINEERS
THE BEACH HOTEL

THE BEACH C1955 B130054
Before the package tour era, English seaside resorts enjoyed a last golden age as England emerged from the austerity that followed World War II. Scenes like this, with families enjoying themselves on full beaches, seem now a distant memory from my childhood.

THE PIER 1955 B130043
Ten years after this happy view was taken, the 1900 end pavilion collapsed into the sea one stormy night. More recently, the tall pedimented part of the shore-end building was removed, along with the balconies and wind-screens, and then a further section of the venerable pier was lost in storms.

Pier Head Gardens c1955 B130027

Pier Head Gardens were formed from the south end of Waterloo Square after the council acquired it in 1921: a municipalising process that has visually totally disrupted the way the pier was centred on the Square. It is sad, too, that the cupola has now gone from the pier building.

Waterloo Gardens c1955 B130046

Behind the Diamond Jubilee Fountain, here in its second home, are four 1820s stucco villas, the earliest on the west side of the square. To the right is the tower of old St John's church, demolished in the 1960s after the church itself had gone in 1892.

WATERLOO GARDENS c1955 B130047
This view is taken to the right of the Diamond Jubilee Fountain in what is now a mini-golf park. The hedge in the middle ground marks the footpath across the Square, behind which are the two bowls greens, opened in 1926, taking up the rest of what had been open greensward.

Esplanade Gardens c1960 B130172
This view was taken in the triangular gardens in front of The Esplanade Theatre, demolished in 1980, and now the Esplanade Skate Park for skate-boarders. It had started with a small bandstand in 1901, which was replaced by a horse-shoe shaped band enclosure in 1937. Roofed in 1947, it became the famed Esplanade Theatre.

The Marine Gardens, Sun Loggia c1955 B130032
Further west and well beyond Park Terrace are The Marine Gardens. Long and rectangular, well hedged and walled, they are peaceful and away from the windy promenade. The western gardens have several of these 1930s sun loggias surviving, although the glazing has since been removed.

MARINE PARADE GARDENS c1960 B130166

Opened in 1935, the gardens are surrounded by 1930s housing from the westward development of Bognor along the Aldwick Road. This view is in the eastern garden, and the loggias and public toilets behind the far loggia survive intact. The 1960s flats beyond fail to detract from the gardens.

THE PROMENADE c1960 B130175

In 1960, much of what had given Bognor its architectural character as an early seaside resort still remained, including Rock Buildings, the 1804 shallow crescent of eleven good stucco houses. It is worrying that it was in the heritage-conscious 1980s that they fell to the bulldozer.

THE BEACH AND PROMENADE, FROM THE PIER c1955 B130056
Since the earlier 1914 view in Chapter 3, the (now demolished) white painted amusement arcade has been built, while beyond The Carlton and Beaulieu Hotels, between them and the Kursaal, was Bognor Zoo, opened in 1933 by Billy Butlin. Later it became a stretch of tearooms and cafes.

THE BEACH FROM THE PIER, LOOKING EAST c1960 B130161
In this view the Kursaal's domed towers gleam in the warm sunshine. However, it and all the other buildings visible have been swept away. Only the white painted bastion out from the promenade into the beach in front of the Kursaal survives as a point of reference!

THE BEACH FROM THE PIER c1960 B130159
This is indeed a nostalgic view of the sea front. Only Colebrooke Terrace beyond the Kursaal's domed towers has gone, to give a view of the rear of Cowles-Voysey's neo-Georgian Town Hall of 1929. The Carlton Hotel's cement render has been painted since the 1955 photograph.

THE MERCHANT TAYLORS HOME AND GARDENS c1955 B130021
These gardens survive, which were formerly the site of Hothampton Place, demolished in 1935. But East Row, later the Merchant Taylors Home, another of Hotham's key buildings, was demolished in 1955, being replaced by the truly awful Fitzleet House: modern houses and shops topped off by a 16 storey block of flats.

THE BEACH FROM THE PIER
Looking North-West c1955 B130069
This view has changed remarkably little since 1900: the only real changes since have been the rebuilding of the sea-wall and promenade, and the glazed dining room extensions added to The Royal Hotel's Grillroom. At the far left can be seen The Esplanade Theatre, demolished in 1980.

PIXIES
PRIVATE HOTEL
Pixies

YORK ROAD

c1955 B130051

Seen from the Promenade, this view shows the bustle of York Road, nowadays a sadly truncated road with only the far section beyond Belmont Street intact. To the right is the side of the Kursaal with its domes and glazed verandah to the shops - now all gone.

ESTATE AGENTS
HOWARDS
BUSINESS AGENCY
ICES

Index

Frith Book Co 1999 Titles

From 2000 we aim at publishing 100 new books each year. For latest catalogue please contact Frith Book Co

Title	ISBN	Price	Date
Barnstaple	1-85937-084-5	£12.99	Oct 99
Blackpool	1-85937-049-7	£12.99	Sep 99
Bognor Regis	1-85937-055-1	£12.99	Sep 99
Bristol	1-85937-050-0	£12.99	Sep 99
Cambridge	1-85937-092-6	£12.99	Oct 99
Cambridgeshire	1-85937-086-1	£14.99	Nov 99
Cheshire	1-85937-045-4	£14.99	Sep 99
Chester	1-85937-090-X	£12.99	Nov 99
Chesterfield	1-85937-071-3	£12.99	Sep 99
Chichester	1-85937-089-6	£12.99	Nov 99
Cornwall	1-85937-054-3	£14.99	Sep 99
Cotswolds	1-85937-099-3	£14.99	Nov 99

Title	ISBN	Price	Date
Derby	1-85937-046-2	£12.99	Sep 99
Devon	1-85937-052-7	£14.99	Sep 99
Dorset	1-85937-075-6	£14.99	Oct 99
Dorset Coast	1-85937-062-4	£14.99	Sep 99
Dublin	1-85937-058-6	£12.99	Sep 99
East Anglia	1-85937-059-4	£14.99	Sep 99
Eastbourne	1-85937-061-6	£12.99	Sep 99
English Castles	1-85937-078-0	£14.99	Oct 99
Essex	1-85937-082-9	£14.99	Nov 99
Falmouth	1-85937-066-7	£12.99	Sep 99
Hampshire	1-85937-064-0	£14.99	Sep 99
Hertfordshire	1-85937-079-9	£14.99	Nov 99
Isle of Man	1-85937-065-9	£14.99	Sep 99
Liverpool	1-85937-051-9	£12.99	Sep 99
Maidstone	1-85937-056-X	£12.99	Sep 99
Northumberland & Tyne and Wear	1-85937-072-1	£14.99	Sep 99
North Yorkshire	1-85937-048-9	£14.99	Sep 99
Nottingham	1-85937-060-8	£12.99	Sep 99
Oxfordshire	1-85937-076-4	£14.99	Oct 99
Penzance	1-85937-069-1	£12.99	Sep 99
Reading	1-85937-087-X	£12.99	Nov 99
St Ives	1-85937-068-3	£12.99	Sep 99
Salisbury	1-85937-091-8	£12.99	Nov 99
Scarborough	1-85937-104-3	£12.99	Sep 99
Scottish Castles	1-85937-077-2	£14.99	Oct 99
Sevenoaks and Tonbridge	1-85937-057-8	£12.99	Sep 99
Sheffield and S Yorkshire	1-85937-070-5	£12.99	Sep 99
Shropshire	1-85937-083-7	£14.99	Nov 99
Southampton	1-85937-088-8	£12.99	Nov 99
Staffordshire	1-85937-047-0	£14.99	Sep 99
Stratford upon Avon	1-85937-098-5	£12.99	Nov 99
Suffolk	1-85937-074-8	£14.99	Oct 99
Surrey	1-85937-081-0	£14.99	Oct 99
Torbay	1-85937-063-2	£12.99	Sep 99
Wiltshire	1-85937-053-5	£14.99	Sep 99

British Life A Century Ago
246 x 189mm
144pp, hardback.
Black and white
Lavishly illustrated with photos from the turn of the century, and with extensive commentary. It offers a unique insight into the social history and heritage of bygone Britain.

1-85937-103-5 £17.99 ....

Available from your local bookshop or from the publisher

FRITH PRODUCTS & SERVICES

Francis Frith would doubtless be pleased to know that the pioneering publishing venture he started in 1860 still continues today. More than a hundred and thirty years later, The Francis Frith Collection continues in the same innovative tradition and is now one of the foremost publishers of vintage photographs in the world. Some of the current activities include:

Interior Decoration

Today Frith's photographs can be seen framed and as giant wall murals in thousands of pubs, restaurants, hotels, banks, retail stores and other public buildings throughout the country. In every case they enhance the unique local atmosphere of the places they depict and provide reminders of gentler days in an increasingly busy and frenetic world.

Product Promotions

Frith products have been used by many major companies to promote the sales of their own products or to reinforce their own history and heritage. Brands include Hovis bread, Courage beers, Scots Porage Oats, Colman's mustard, Cadbury's foods, Mellow Birds coffee, Dunhill pipe tobacco, Guinness, and Bulmer's Cider.

Genealogy and Family History

As the interest in family history and roots grows world-wide, more and more people are turning to Frith's photographs of Great Britain for images of the towns, villages and streets where their ancestors lived; and, of course, photographs of the churches and chapels where their ancestors were christened, married and buried are an essential part of every genealogy tree and family album.
A series of easy-to-use CD Roms is planned for publication, and an increasing number of Frith photographs will be able to be viewed on specialist genealogy sites. A growing range of Frith books will be available on CD.

The Internet

Already thousands of Frith photographs can be viewed and purchased on the internet. By the end of the year 2000 some 60,000 Frith photographs will be available on the internet. The number of sites is constantly expanding, each focussing on different products and services from the Collection.
Some of the sites are listed below.

www.townpages.co.uk
www.familystorehouse.com
www.britannia.com
www.icollector.com
www.barclaysquare.co.uk
www.cornwall-online.co.uk

For background information on the Collection look at the two following sites:

www.francisfrith.com
www.francisfrith.co.uk

Frith Products

All Frith photographs are available Framed or just as Mounted Prints, and can be ordered from the address below. From time to time other products - Address Books, Calendars, Table Mats, Postcards etc - are available.

The Frith Collectors' Guild

In response to the many customers who enjoy collecting Frith photographs we have created the Frith Collectors' Guild. Members are entitled to a range of benefits, including a regular magazine, special discounts and special limited edition products.

For further information: if you would like further information on any of the above aspects of the Frith business please contact us at the address below:

The Francis Frith Collection, Frith's Barn, Teffont, Salisbury, Wiltshire England SP3 5QP.
Tel: +44 (0) 1722 716 376 Fax: +44 (0) 1722 716 881 Email: frithbook.co.uk

To receive your FREE Mounted Print

Cut out this Voucher and return it with your remittance for £1.50 to cover postage and handling. Choose any photograph included in this book. Your SEPIA print will be A4 in size, and mounted in a cream mount with burgundy rule lines, overall size 14 x 11 inches.

Order additional Mounted Prints at HALF PRICE (only £7.49 each*)
If there are further pictures you would like to order, possibly as gifts for friends and family, acquire them at half price (no additional postage and handling required).

Have your Mounted Prints framed*
For an additional £14.95 per print you can have your chosen Mounted Print framed in an elegant polished wood and gilt moulding, overall size 16 x 13 inches (no additional postage and handling required).

*** IMPORTANT!**
These special prices are only available if ordered using the original voucher on this page (no copies permitted) and at the same time as your free Mounted Print, for delivery to the same address

for FREE and Reduced Price Frith Prints

Picture no.	Page number	Qty	Mounted @ £7.49	Framed + £14.95	Total Cost
		1	**Free of charge***	£	£
			£	£	£
			£	£	£
			£	£	£
			£	£	£
			£	£	£
				* Post & handling	£1.50
				Total Order Cost	**£**

Title: AROUND BOGNOR
055-1

Please do not photocopy this voucher. Only the original is valid, so please cut it out and return it to us.

I enclose a cheque / postal order for £ . . . .
made payable to 'The Francis Frith Collection'
OR please debit my Mastercard / Visa / Switch / Amex card

Number . . . .

Expires . . . . Signature . . . .

Name Mr/Mrs/Ms ....

Address ....

....

....

....

.... Postcode ....

Daytime Tel No .... Valid to 31/12/01

Frith Collectors' Guild

From time to time we publish a magazine of news and stories about Frith photographs and further special offers of Frith products. If you would like 12 months FREE membership, please return this form and we will send you a New Member Pack.

The Francis Frith Collectors' Guild

I would like to receive the New Members Pack offering 12 months FREE membership.

055-1

Name Mr/Mrs/Ms ....

Address ....

....

....

.... Postcode ....

Send completed forms to:
The Francis Frith Collection, Frith's Barn, Teffont, Salisbury, Wiltshire SP3 5QP